642

TINY THINGS TO
WRITE ABOUT

BY THE SAN FRANCISCO
WRITERS' GROTTO
INTRODUCTION BY PO BRONSON

D1026235

CHRONICLE BOOKS
SAN FRANCISCO

CONTRIBUTORS

Marie Baca	Rachel Levin
Tom Barbash	Stephanie Losee
JD Beltran	Laura McClure
Liza Boyd	David Munro
Po Bronson	Caroline Paul
Marianna Cherry	Bridget Quinn
Lindsey Crittenden	Jason Roberts
Ali Eteraz	Ethel Rohan
Yalitza Ferreras	Lorraine Sanders
Alastair Gee	Julia Scheeres
Susie Gerhard	Lavinia Spalding
Lisa Gray	Lizette Wanzer
Jeff Greenwald	Meghan Ward
Justine Gubar	Ethan Watters
Vanessa Hua	Maw Shein Win
Yukari Kane	Emily Wolahan
Diana Kapp	Maury Zeff
Renae Lesser	

Library of Congress Cataloging-in-Publication Data available.

ISBN: 978-1-4521-4217-3

Manufactured in China

Designed by Tatiana Pavlova

10 9 8 7 6 5 4

Chronicle Books LLC
680 Second Street
San Francisco, California 94107
www.chroniclebooks.com

This tiny book contains all the ingredients
to expand your mind, make time disappear,
and supercharge your creativity.

Except you'll also need a pen.

Enjoy,

PO BRONSON
San Francisco Writers' Grotto

Write yesterday's fortune cookie.
It got everything wrong.

Write last year's fortune cookie.
It got everything right.

Boil down *Hamlet*, Shakespeare's longest play, to a tweet (140 characters).

Now tweet the plot of the original *Star Wars*.

Tweet the story of your life.

Tweet your day, so far.

Write about a time you broke:

A bone

A heart

The law

A promise

Think about your weirdest family member and write one short scene that depicts why he or she is such an oddball.

You accidentally hit Reply All—and everyone
received an uncensored rant about your boss.
Write the follow-up Reply All.

Where would you choose to be exiled?

What three essential items would you take with you?

Describe your first kiss.

Describe your most recent kiss.

Describe your next kiss.

Write instructions for how to do something you haven't learned to do since you were very young (blow a bubblegum bubble, or swim, or tie your shoes, or make a paper airplane, or build a snowman, for instance).

At a banquet in Kazakhstan, you are greeted as a guest of honor and served the traditional sheep's eyeball. Respectfully, you decline. You are then offered the sheep's tongue, instead. What's your excuse this time?

Write the first sentence of a feature profile of you
in a men's fashion magazine.

Write the first sentence of a feature profile of you
in a business magazine.

Write the first sentence of your obituary.

The woman/man across from you at a café or cubicle:
What did she or he dream last night?

You are being held at gunpoint, and your assailant
says you have 10 seconds to make him/her change
their mind about shooting you. What do you say?

Think of one dramatic event from your life
(an accident, a fight, a loss) and write
the event backward.

Describe the sounds of the street outside your office building the moment after you were fired and escorted from the building.

_____

_____

_____

_____

_____

_____

_____

_____

_____

_____

_____

You wake up one morning to find your face plastered
all over town on a "Missing" poster.
Who posted the signs?

Where were you last seen?

What were you wearing?

George Washington sits in on a session of Congress, 2014. He writes a quick postcard to his wife. What does it say?

Pretend you're a tree. What are you thinking as they try to cut you down?

You live in a cloud. Give three tips for
how not to fall off.

As a talking Chihuahua, what would you tell your
humans about the new crying baby who now
lives with you?

Your mom has started online dating. She's going out
on four or five dates a week, splitting her time
among three men. She wants to tell you
more about it than you want to hear.
For each man, describe in her words the
details that make you uncomfortable.

1.

2.

3.

College application time. Explain in one paragraph
why you want to attend a historical black college.

Your character has an unusual first date:

With whom? Make it strange.

Why? Make it strange.

How's the first kiss? Make it strange.

What's the second date? Make it strange.

Think of your worst rejection. Write a thank-you
note to the person who rejected you.

A fast-spreading virus knocks out people's capacity for anger. Half the city is infected. How does this make life worse?

Find a photo and write what's not in the picture.

Write the headline of an online dating profile for the man who just walked by you.

"Statement necklaces" are the fashion. What statement about you does your necklace make?

Outline the plot turns for the personal history of
one of your most treasured objects.

_____

_____

_____

_____

_____

_____

_____

_____

_____

_____

_____

Your partner just suggested that you both be allowed to see other people on the side. Who do you suspect your partner has in mind?

You loaned your car to a friend, forgetting that there's something stashed in there you don't want anybody to find. What is it?

A foreign exchange student is spending
a week with you.
What is the one restaurant you want to
take the student to?

The one scenic spot?

The one person you want the student to meet?

Write the P.S. note for a resignation letter.

Write the P.S. note for the last letter ever sent
from one human to another.

We all have junk.
List the items in your fridge that you never use.

Describe a shirt in your closet
that you never wear.

What's in your basement that you just
can't throw out?

When your character was in third grade, he wore the same comfy shirt every single day. Describe it.

Someone parked his or her car in a way that makes it hard for you to exit your garage.
Write a very nice note.

Write a very angry note.

Name the model and a key detail of your first car.

Name the model and a key detail of your current car.

Name the model and key details of the car
you would design.

Write the opening line of your solo show.

A genie grants you three tiny wishes.
What are they?

What the person nearest you at this very second is
really thinking about

Write why the giant wishes he were small.

You have an app that monitors your boss's mood.

What's it called?   Your husband/wife/
                                     partner's?

Your daughter/son's?   Your mom's?

In your office fridge, an angry note
left by a coworker

At a speed-dating event, he felt he'd maybe met
"the One," despite only 60 seconds together. Why?

You see your old girlfriend at the gas station. She tells you she's moving away to Tennessee with her husband. Her nine-year-old-son is in the car. He's never known that you're his real father. What's the boy doing, right then, sitting in the car?

You've made a documentary about the biggest crisis in the life of the family that raised you. It debuts at Sundance, and the first question from the audience is, "What inspired you to actually tell this story now?"

Write an answer.

The second question is: "Who funded this film?"

The third question is: "How did you come up with the title?"

The fourth question is: "Have your parents seen it?"

Explain why ice cream is better than gelato.

Why gelato is better than ice cream

Why coffee is better than tea

Why tea is better than coffee

The letter in your office mailbox is from your
high school boyfriend—your first true love,
25 years ago. The return address is Osaka, Japan.
Your office mates are dying to know what it says.
What do you tell them?

An undercover spy is about to impersonate you in all aspects of your life. Write instructions.

Write 20 words about your first:
Car

Job

Apartment

Write a scene in which a character understands that a good friend has lost his or her mind.

Someone apartment-sitting learns three unsettling things about the inhabitant of the apartment.

Plot a story about a disastrous vacation involving two families in the same house.

You're visiting the top-secret facilities of a candy conglomerate when you open an unmarked door. As alarms start going off, you notice . . .

On your old family farm there's an oak tree with a big rusty chain around it. What used to be chained to the tree?

Your senator has been embezzling money.
Write him an outraged letter.

Write him a letter of sympathy.

Quickly, argue why independent films are better
than Hollywood blockbusters.

Now argue why Hollywood blockbusters are better
than independent films.

Because of your assistance in a case against a
mobster, you and your family must now choose:
A new place to live

An identity in that new place

Explain to a child why evolution is totally
illogical and laughable.

Explain to that same child why creationism is
totally illogical and laughable.

Now matter-of-factly explain to her where life
on Earth really originated.

Write your life story in five sentences.

What's most surprising when your character:

Loses the use of her
right arm.

Loses the use of
both legs.

Loses the use of the
left side of her face.

Loses the power to see.

Your favorite authors and your favorite musicians
are playing a baseball game against each other.
Describe the winning play.

In the neighbor's driveway is a pickup truck. Three
details about this truck make you worry someone is
back in town, and there's trouble ahead.
What are the three details?

Who is back in town?

Someone completely unexpected comes out of the
house and drives away in the car. Who was it?

As CEO you have to write an apology for your company's defective product.

Barack Obama meets Martin Luther King Jr.
What do they talk about?

Bill Gates meets Andrew Carnegie.
What do they talk about?

Carl Sagan meets Plato.
What do they talk about?

Dante Aligheri (*Inferno*):
"Midway on our life's journey, I found myself
In dark woods, the right road lost."
You:
Write the opening line to an epic poem about your
life, and everything.

Imagine you cut someone off while driving on the road. Write that person an apology.

Sophomore English 2.0. Without looking at the book, try to recall or reinvent the first sentence of Camus's *The Stranger*.

Now for Fitzgerald's *The Great Gatsby*

Lee's *To Kill a Mockingbird*

Bradbury's *Fahrenheit 451*

Three ways you and your sibling are
totally different

Three ways you and that same sibling
are totally the same

Think about your best friend. He or she knocks on your door tonight in a panic, and needs to make a desperate confession. Then, unable to say it, your friend runs away. What do you think it probably is?

What do you most fear it is?

What is it unlikely, but not impossible, to be?

What did your hair say about you in middle school?

What did your hair say about you in college?

What does your hair say about you now?

If you were a graffiti artist, what
would your tag be?

If you were a rapper, what would you call yourself?

There is a message on your voice mail that will change your life for the better.

There is a message on your voice mail that will change your life for the worse.

A Unitarian minister has just been spited by his
girlfriend. Write the first few lines of
his Sunday sermon.

What do the Post-it note reminders say on the desks
of the following people:
The President of the United States

Dumbledore

God

Your favorite part of your lover's body

Your least favorite part of your lover's body

You get home and your spouse says, "We need to talk." The first thing that flashes through your mind is . . .

You're going to die next week, and you need to destroy a few things before your family finds them. What?

Aloha! You're a lost tourist on a locals-only beach in Hawaii. Talk your way out of a night mugging, using only surfer slang and sea turtle metaphors.

You made the first machine that turns water into gold. You've got one minute to pitch investors on what your machine is. Go.

Your mother is dying, and you need to clear the air about . . .

You spot your best friend's spouse kissing another person. What are the first three things you do?

Pick a state you've never been to. Explain why
you are moving there.

Give us the first sentence of these stories:
You're walking down a quiet street and you notice
a body lying in the gutter. You don't know if the
person is dead or alive.

You come across that same motionless body—and you
notice a wallet sticking out from under it.

Now it's a gun sticking out.

Describe the most gruesome thing you've ever
seen or experienced.

Consider your oldest friendship. Describe how you
could destroy it in five minutes.

Think of a big mistake you've made. Write a scene in which you either repair that mistake, or do it over differently.

Find a picture from when you were a toddler. Write about that moment from the perspective of your child self.

Think about your day so far (even if it's still morning). What's the highlight at this point?

What's the low point?

Come up with an imaginative nickname for your boss.

Come up with an imaginative nickname for your
least favorite person.

Come up with a nickname for the stranger at your
gym/café/bus/work who you see all the time.

Someone you dislike asks you to lunch. You've just made a pact with yourself to be brutally honest in your life. What do you say?

Write the instructions for breaking up with a boyfriend, as if it were driving directions to the airport.

After she started working full-time downtown,
her personality totally changed.

Write the confession of a man who killed his
best friend by accident.

Write the confession of a man who killed his best
friend in a drunken bar fight over a spilled
drink, and who repents.

Write the confession of a man who killed his best
friend and is not sorry at all.

You come home from a cousin's wedding, where
something went tragically wrong. But you're
secretly happy that at least something
interesting happened. What was it?

You're a winemaker. Describe the wine you're
pricing at $100 a bottle.

Now, the one you're pricing at $1,000 a bottle.

Now, the one you're selling for five bucks.
(By the way, all three are the same wine.)

Ever since you visited a website about government
satellites, you've been getting strange
e-mails like this one.

Write the first paragraph in an emergency presidential speech about going to war.

About the death of the vice-president

About the bottom suddenly falling out of the economy

About the president's sudden resignation

Santa's reindeer were named Dasher, Dancer,
Prancer, Vixen, Comet, Cupid, Donner, Blitzen, and
Rudolph. Rename them all as Satan's reindeer.

Your roommate is out on a Saturday night. There's
a knock on your door. It's your roommate's father,
a little tipsy. Being hospitable, you let him in.
Slowly, he tries to persuade you of something.
What is it?

You start an online petition to move the international date line from the Pacific to the Atlantic Ocean.

You need 100,000 signatures to get your item on the ballot. What is your main argument in favor of this?

You make contact with Earth's first alien visitors,
and they ask you the best place to land.
What do you tell them?

What does Neil deGrasse Tyson tell them?

What does Keith Richards tell them?

What's a better way to say:

Boring   Uncomfortable

Pretty   Slippery

Fill in the blanks.

One day, I went to ____'s house for lunch. She served _____. I thought it would taste like _____, but it tasted like _____. *Bleh.*

Now find a way to compliment the chef in the situation just described.

You've just heard that your favorite potato chip flavor will no longer be available. Write an indignant letter to the manufacturer.

Frankenstein's best actor acceptance speech

You open your fridge and realize someone has replaced all your food with things you hate to eat. Describe what's in there.

Who did this and why?

You're accompanying a class of 11-year-olds on a field trip to the science museum. In the gift shop, you notice one of them slipping a toy into his pocket.

Imagine now that you notice as the boy breaks one of the expensive sale objects, but then puts it back, hoping no one noticed.

Imagine seeing that same boy pick another customer's pocket.

Describe a moment or event that made you either
more or less religious or spiritual.

In your wallet is a $20 bill with this written on
the white trim along the bottom:

In your wallet is a short letter that your
grandfather gave to your father. It reads . . .

Even killers have junk in their glove compartment.
You've been stopped by a cop for speeding.

What is your best excuse, hoping to elude a ticket?

Write about something you stole.

Write about a lie you told.

Write about catching someone else in a lie.

An out-of-office, vacation auto-response, as
written by Ernest Hemingway

An Evite to Oscar Wilde's reading

Describe the morning light glinting off the ice along the highway's edge as you drive home to confess where you've been all night.

In a sentence, describe the smell of spring.

In a word, the sound of winter

In a line of a limerick, the feel of fall

In five words, the taste of summer

Tell a kid what these movies are about in
one sentence.

Casablanca

A River Runs Through It

Field of Dreams

*How the Grinch Stole
Christmas*

A skeleton of an ancient dinosaur has just been uncovered during construction of a new subway line. Describe the characteristics of this animal when it was alive.

You're a pathological liar. Write a paragraph
confessing this to your friends.

Here's the formula: H + 2W = L
What does it mean?

Your dog senses something is not right in the
family, but you don't know what it is, and
the dog can't talk.

You return to your childhood hometown.
Who is the person you want to see most?

The person you want to see least?

The memory you'd most like to relive?

A Beatles song as rap lyrics

A boy snooping through his mother's closet finds a
box on a high shelf. Inside, he uncovers _____.
Name four possibilities and the
different outcomes.

Walking into a party, you spot the ex you've been avoiding (and dreading seeing, and secretly wanting to see) for years, walking toward you.
Write the conversation.

You've just been informed you must leave the country and not look back or contact anyone you know for a year. You're allowed to fill one suitcase. List the contents of your getaway bag.

Write your short acceptance speech for:
An Academy Award

The Pulitzer

The Nobel Peace Prize

I buried it in the backyard. *(What?)*

My _____ dug it up. *(Who?)*

From there, it fell into the wrong hands. *(Where did it go?)*

The blowback on me was, shall we say, awkward. *(What were the consequences?)*

You're divorcing your spouse. Rewrite your
wedding vows.

A pep talk from a coach who is dead certain his
team is going to lose the big game.

Describe the word *psychedelic* to a friend
who is learning English.

New Year's Eve in Abu Dhabi

Define *brevity*, in brief.

A teenage girl looks up the Internet browser
history on her father's computer and is shocked to
discover _____. Name four sites.

Your mother-in-law asks to move in. Email her back
why this wouldn't be a good idea.

Write the first communication sent back to Earth
after humans land on Mars.

Write a headline for the day after the world ends.

You're launching a sound recording of life on Earth into outer space to act as an emissary for the human race. Name the five specific sounds you will record.

Convey the third sound in detail. Don't bother using words.

Your recording may include a short inscription on it, the only text that will accompany these Earth sounds. There is space for only six words.

Write a haiku about your favorite food.

Write a haiku about your favorite sport.

Your last word before you die

Plot a story in which the drama hangs on a stolen pair of socks.

Which is the oldest tree in your neighborhood, and what has it seen?

Your dad's in a rock band. What is it called?

Write the title of your autobiography.

What is your tiny pearl of wisdom?

Find a passage in your favorite novel. Re-tell it, using only one-syllable words.

Write an alternate ending for *It's a Wonderful Life*.

Explain why you've given this famous restaurant only one star—even though you've never eaten there.

You're a student career counselor at a reputable state university. A 21-year-old neuroscience major tells you she wants to switch to become an art major. Describe what you'd say if:
Your job were to steer her back to neuroscience.

Your job were to just give the facts of which art classes needed to be taken.

Your father were a prominent commercial artist who made plenty of money but was never happy.

The game is telephone. A gangly teen starts it off. He says . . .

But his annoyed-to-be-playing sister hears . . .

When she passes it off to their flighty cousin visiting from South Carolina, she hears . . .

The hard-of-hearing grandpa thought she said . . .

Around her neck was a tiny, spinning prayer wheel, and
inside it, under the petite peaked top, was a miniature
scroll. On it, in teeny print, it said . . .

Write a menu for a feast fit for the gods
on Mount Olympus.

You're a statue in a city park. Describe what you see in each of the four seasons.

Winter

Spring

Summer

Fall

The want ad for a young couple seeking a
surrogate grandparent

A note in a bottle you found washed up on the shores
of Disney World's Lake Buena Vista water park

Once upon a time, there was a (ADJECTIVE_____)
wrestler named Tiny. One day, Tiny was (VERB
ending in -*ing*_____) near the White House when an
enormous (NOUN_____) fell on Tiny's head. Because
of that, Tiny was forever (ADVERB_____). For some
reason, no one investigated. (END THE STORY.)

Write about a time when one or both of your parents:

Disciplined you   Rewarded you

Embarrassed you   Made you proud

If you were given one extra hour today and you weren't allowed to use it for anything you'd normally do (e.g., eat, sleep, exercise, work, watch TV, or play on the Internet,), what would you do with that hour?

Your archenemy is dying of cancer; write
her a get-well card.

Write the first line of your wedding vows, as if
you were marrying:

Your dentist

Your stalker

Your ex-wife or
ex-husband

A complete stranger

It's 1849, and you're headed west along the Oregon
Trail. Describe the safety features of your
state-of-the-art covered wagon.

There's a knock on your door.
What is the caller selling?

What are three tools you cannot live without?

The name of the café where they first met

Write a one-paragraph treatment for a TV reality show set in your workplace.

"This is 911. What is your emergency?"

The smell of an orange reminds me of . . .

When I smell Pine Sol, I think of . . .

You're looking into a bottomless pit. Describe your reactions:

As you first look into the pit

As you trip and fall in

Five minutes later

Three days later

Your son (or daughter) sits you down and tells you
that s/he has agreed to be one of the
first colonists on Mars.

You are leafing through a book of portraits of well-known people in ecstasy. Describe the expressions of:

George Washington | Attila the Hun

Catherine the Great | Napoleon Bonaparte

You see a clown on the bus and flash back to the party where, when you were a kid, one scared the crap out of you, literally. This is your chance to get even before you get off the bus. What do you do?

Think what you ate for breakfast this morning.
Write a recipe for how to prepare it.

What started a centuries-old blood feud?

In the conversation you wish you'd never had,
you said . . .

Your first and your most recent lover meet.

What is number three in your top list of places you
want to go?

Write a breakup text to yourself.

What are five key words in your manifesto?

Which finger are you most like—pinky, middle,
pointer, ring, or thumb—and why?

How does someone with your name look and act?

If you could time-travel to last week, for one hour, what would you do?

You administer a microloan program for Cuban women in Miami. You discover your boss has been "lending" money to himself. Write the confrontation dialogue.

Fill in the blanks and keep going. A popular freshman boy spots his geeky older sister at school wearing his letterman's jacket. As they pass each other in the hallway, _____.

Today I went to the zoo with my toddler. We saw a _____ and a _____, but nothing could top when the _____ escaped! We hid in the _____ until we heard _____.

It's January and you give away the puppy your son
got for the holidays.

Why?

What do you tell your
son/everyone?

What's the strangest
thing that happens
next?

What's the funniest
thing that happens
next?

The home from your favorite fairy tale is now up for sale (the gingerbread house from Hansel and Gretel, Bluebeard's castle, etc.). Write a quick description of the house for the real estate listing.

Write the liner notes for the lost, final album
of your favorite band.

Retitle five of your favorite books.

Rename five constellations.

The local school board has just done something to
really tick you off. What is it?

There's a note on a table, and lots of blood.
What happened?

Tell us about something surprising that happened to you recently, in one paragraph.

Now tell us about it in a Facebook post.

Tell us about it in a tweet.

Write about a time you were in trouble with your parents, or school principal or teacher, or the law, but write it from the point of view of the person in authority.

Write the key line of a convocation graduation speech you will be giving to 100 preschoolers going off to kindergarten.

One morning you run into the person who bullied you in grade school. After the preliminary greetings, you let loose. What do you say?

There's a new cleanse diet. Explain why berries are OK but bananas and apples aren't.

Describe "impure thoughts."

Define "infidelity."

Come up with names for five different haircuts.

Starbucks, the global coffee chain, was almost dubbed *Pequod*, for the sailing ship from the novel *Moby Dick*, and was instead named after the *Pequod's* chief mate, to evoke the seafaring tradition of early coffee traders. Invent another brand name taken from a classic novel.

"Within the four seas, all men are brothers," according to the classic Chinese novel *Water Margin*, whose bandit-heroes include Iron Arm, Leaping Tiger, Nimble Monkey, and Suppressor of Three Mountains. Invent the names of four heroes and their powers.

In the Beatles archetype theory, groups of four fall into the same pattern of personality and interpersonal dynamic as John, Paul, George, and Ringo. In a family of four, describe who takes each role.

The John personality	The Paul personality
The George personality	**The Ringo personality**

Describe the perfect job for you, even if
it doesn't exist yet.

A sympathy card for the Devil

Your very unusual allergy

Write about going broke.

The next sentence of a story that begins: "Yeah, he was wearing a wedding ring, but so was I."

Five punch lines in search of a setup

Graffiti in the White House bathroom

The menu for your last meal

British scientists germinated 200-year-old seeds from a Dutch merchant who'd collected them on a trip to the Cape of Good Hope. Though they've identified many of the sprouted plants, one remains a mystery until it flowers. Describe the flower and give it a name.

You call in sick to go to a nude hot springs (or beach) and run into your boss. Describe the scene.

Make a Top-Five list of the details God is in.

Describe Earth to an _____ alien—
25 words or less.

List the items on the credit card statement of the
cheating spouse.

Pick any story from today's newspaper. Tomorrow,
the story turns in a radically unexpected way.
What happens?

Randomly choose a word or phrase in a foreign
language that you don't know, and write
a translation.

In this world, when you turn 18 you are sent an envelope with the name of the one person on the planet you must meet and get to know. Who is your person, how do you meet, and what happens next?

In chaos theory, a small change can lead to a large one later. A distant butterfly flapping its wings can launch a hurricane. Apply the butterfly effect to complete this sentence: If I caught the earlier bus, then _____.

Fill in the blanks and keep going: I was taking the bus when I suddenly saw _____, who started to _____.

She was rafting downriver when her boat flipped, and she was sucked down into the rapids for two minutes, unable to escape. At death's door, she heard a voice; then the water released her. From then on, she lived her life differently. What did the voice say?

Though it was fun as a kid, now that he's an adult,
he really hates being an identical twin. What bugs
him the most about his twin brother?

Your lover has organized the perfect date night.
Describe the perfect setting.

The perfect food

The perfect ending

You're an astronaut about to exit your space capsule and take the first steps on a distant planet. What stirring words do you send back to Earth?

Best snack food of the past century

Best snack food of the future

Invent a new beverage and name it.

Write a letter to the editor explaining why the
"Letters to the Editor" section of their
magazine should be abolished.

Due to political machinations, the country
you came from no longer exists.
What's different now?

What's the same?

You see your eighty-year-old self on the beach in
Hawaii; you're twenty. What four questions do
you ask about sex and relationships?

You're an acrobat in a flea circus. Describe your
signature move and its name.

"___!" she shouted, after she jumped off the _____
with her _____.

Write a one-line ad for a rubber band.

Your day in a hashtag

Her true colors were revealed that day, when she . . .

You start an intergalactic dating website.
What do you name it?

You need to fire the CEO of your company. She's gotten great performance reviews, but she lacks "soft" skills. You write a one-paragraph severance letter. What does it say?

How's it going? Write the honest answer.

Write a conspiracy theory involving multiple
countries and individuals regarding the
disappearance of your soap.

Write descriptively about food.
What was the worst thing your parents ever
made you eat?

What's the best meal you remember?

If you had to choose one final food of your
life, what would it be?

What did your seventh-grade math teacher wear?

Seventh-grade English teacher?

Seventh-grade Sex Ed teacher?

You are an ancient Roman. You ventured to Pompeii, Italy, two weeks after the volcanic eruption of Vesuvius. Bear witness for people back home.

A new (and ridiculous) food trend hits big cities.
What is it? Write the menu description for this
signature dish.

What was your favorite flavor of ice cream
as a child, and why?

What's your favorite flavor now?

What flavor have you always wanted to invent?

What is written on the postcard that turns up in
your mail from a person you haven't
spoken to in ten years?

Today's weather forecast, if the television station
fired its current talking head and hired a poet

Write a review of your imaginary
autobiography/memoir.

Think of an animal in motion—a bird or cat or
horse—and describe how it moves, action by action.

You—or a character of your invention—are on a plane with your partner, and your relationship is falling apart. You see a former flame/crush/lover. She/he looks great. You make knowing eye contact, and sense that the attraction is mutual. Your partner gets up to the go to the bathroom. Write your former flame a quick note.

Your raffle prize is a skywritten note
over the Super Bowl. *Go.*

Awards you won today for mundane achievements

A sound bite from you meeting your doppelgänger

The first line of a constitution for the new
country you just founded

The line the Wicked Witch scrapped in favor of
"Surrender Dorothy!"

Before the judge passes sentence, what do you want
to tell the court?

In 1962, Decca Records famously turned down the Beatles in their attempt to obtain a recording contract. Write the rejection letter to Brian Epstein, the Beatles' manager.

What does a tattoo removal specialist dream about?

Name some new nail polishes.

What creature would you like to add to
the animal kingdom?

You have a crush on your first cousin. Describe him
or her, injecting your own self-loathing, denial,
and conflictedness about your feelings
into the description.

Due to some family ties, a Yale MBA ends up running a brothel in rural Georgia. Describe the "annual review" meeting he has with one of his employees.

Fill in the blank, then keep going. "In my next life, I wish to be ____."

Mark Twain challenges you to a spelling bee. You get the first two words right, but choke on the third. What is it?

Create a new government agency. Start with the acronym.

Your beloved has had a religious conversion.
He/she is suddenly a devout . . .

The warning label that should come with
first-time parenthood

Write about a visit to the hospital.

You are the world champion at holding your breath.
You can hold your breath for six and a half minutes.
How did you come to have this ability? What now?

The next sentence of a story that begins: "It was midnight and the front door was standing wide open."

Finish this sentence, and then keep going: "It was the first real gift I remember receiving: _____"

You accidentally open your neighbor's mailbox.
What do you find?

Describe a child's hands.

Describe your childhood Christmas tree.

You've just committed a horrific crime. You've stolen a cute, fat baby out of a stroller at the beach and driven home with it. You were acting on a strong impulse; but now you're coming to your senses and you've got to make some hard decisions. What do you do next?

Write a thank-you note to your feet, for some of the places they've taken you.

Now write a thank-you note to your hands, for some of the things they've done for you.

The passenger safety instructions card
for a stage coach

The passenger safety instructions card for
a time-travel machine

How did you find out there was no Santa Claus?

You are a fruit fly but you still have your normal, human mind. You have 24 hours to live. What is on your to-do list for your small, brief life?

Write from the point of view of a person who, after being mistaken for someone else, decides to pretend to be that person.

Your cat or dog is running for political office.
Write its political slogan.

Write four names for a punk rock band.

What do you find in the gutter?

A one-night stand. What is the message left on the nightstand?

Open a manhole cover. What do you see?

Fill in the missing letters:
_ow _uch _ood __ould a _ood_uck _uck if a _ood_uck __ould _uck _ood.

You have been selected to travel on the first manned flight to Mars—a one way trip, with no way to return to Earth. Write a letter to your family saying good-bye.

What piece of advice do you most often
give and least often follow?

Transcribe your dog's thoughts.

A cocktail is named after you. What is it called?

A woman's apartment is robbed, and police have no leads. The following month, she's visiting her parents when she discovers one of the stolen items and _____. What happens next?

Dolphins always keep moving, sleeping with only one
half of the brain at a time. If humans had evolved
this skill, describe a dream you might have.

_____

_____

_____

_____

_____

_____

_____

_____

_____

_____

What was the first sign you knew you were in love?

What was the first sign you had fallen out of love?

Send a toxic friend a breakup text.

Write about the first moment you knew
you could kiss well.

Create three new job titles for your favorite
sports franchise.

You cross the border from Jordan into Saudi Arabia, and see the sign at customs saying "Drug Importation Is Punishable by Beheading." You remember you have a few joints "hidden" in your toiletry case. Describe the bag search.

Write from the viewpoint of someone who loses a child in a crowd.

Invent your own internet meme.

Fill in the blank: If I had a diamond grill, I would
_____.

You're sitting alone on a seemingly deserted beach.
A dog comes running up to you, out of nowhere, and
starts to pull you by the sleeve.

You climb into a taxi in Tehran, Iran. The driver asks you, "Why does America think it is the boss of the whole world?" You reply.

Favorite food court meal from a 1987 mall

Shakespeare had a goldfish. What was its name?

Your least favorite word

Describe the smallest kindest act that someone
has ever done for you.

What was one toy you always wanted as a child
but never actually got to have?

Red or white wine? Why?

After visiting a friend in New York, you are startled to find yourself in an elevator with Henry Kissinger. There's a five-minute blackout. Describe the conversation.

You'll be given five million dollars for your
favorite charity, but first you must
argue its worth.

Your friend shows up with a bad haircut.
What do you say?

Write as many adjectives as you can to describe
the color black.

Write as many adjectives as you can to describe
the color white.

What is at the top of your list of things you want
to do before you die?

The words on your tombstone

You are designing a T-shirt. What does it say?

Shortly after time travel is perfected, you are asked to accompany Benjamin Franklin on his first transcontinental flight. Describe boarding and takeoff. (He has one large carry-on.)

Google William Carlos Williams's poem
"So Much Depends."
Now write your own poem about something
you can see from your window.

You have already published four novels, and
dedicated them to the first four priority persons
in your life. Write the one-phrase/sentence
dedication note for your fifth.

You're invited on a hot air balloon ride.
Why do you say yes?

Why do you say no?

What do you see as you drift over
your neighbor's yard?

Create a greeting card—both the cover
and inside sentiment—

for a divorce.   For a lost pet

For gender reassignment   For winning the lottery
surgery

Give a name to the star you just adopted.

First date: Booth, table, or counter?

Offer a one-sentence argument for who your city
should name its next street after.

You just won the lottery, so you quit the job you hate under the boss who has always been mean to you. Write the resignation letter.

You realize you misread a number and you didn't win the lottery after all. Now you need your job back. Write that letter.

Tweet "Moby Dick."

Describe the color red.

A carrier pigeon brings this tiny note from a
father to a son he's never met.

Your Starbucks coffee order

Describe something about your favorite person that is often underappreciated.

You and Obama are good friends. Write him a text.

You are a preschool teacher. Write a letter of recommendation for one of your students to a private school kindergarten program.

Write the private school's boilerplate rejection letter for kindergarten applicants.

Write an excuse note to the teacher for why your
fourth-grader's Roman Colosseum model
was not completed in time.

Write a note to a mother for why her fourth-grade
child's Roman Colosseum model will not be
put on display at school.

Write a personal ad for your single mother.

Tweet from the POV of God.

How would you split a slice of cake among
five people?

Your mother's most frequent advice

Your father's most frequent advice

A woman's employer moves her to a branch in a
different city. The job is the same—but
the new city makes her really happy.
Where did she move from, and where did she move to?

What's made her life so much better?

Your daughter sees something at the State Fair that
makes her really uncomfortable.
What did she see?

What do you tell her?

Concoct an Internet username and password used by a Latin American studies professor who can't get tenure at the local college.

A new gritty TV drama set in the world of Wall Street needs a name.

Three more ways to say "Oh Shit!"

Why did he run away from home?

Write a one-sentence insult without
any swear words.

His lie would have fooled her, except for one word
that gave him away. What was that word?

Your neighbor's beloved cat died. What condolences
do you give?

What condolences do you give if you dislike your
neighbor?

If you could pass on one line of wisdom to your former self, what would it be?

If you could pass on one line of wisdom to people living 10,000 years in the future, what would it be?

You called the police on your neighbors.
What did she/he do?

The name you would have chosen for yourself

Your mood today in one word

Rewrite the plot of your favorite book into a very short children's book.

You get arrested for painting graffiti on City Hall. The word that put you in the slammer was _____.

Transport Herman Melville to the 21st century. His preferred literary form is ultra-flash fiction.

Describe your job as if it were a hobby.

Describe your hobby as if it were a job.

What incident is forcing you to move
to another planet?

How are you getting there?

The mood you wish you were in, in one word

Your father is retiring. Write a limerick
in his honor.

Create the caption for a cat photo that
will go viral.

It's 2045. Describe a roadside attraction
on the moon.

It's 2018. Where did you last see your jet pack on
Saturday?

Write a paragraph with sentences that are no longer than three words each.

Describe the smell of spring showers.

The last time you saw a dead loved one.

Write the ad for a new breakfast cereal made entirely out of pine bark.

Now, write the recall notice.

What fact have you used to prove a point recently?
Dispute it.

What's in your thought bubble right now?

Your friend invented a new baby sling/carrier, and
you suggested it be called "The _____."
She is not amused.

Beefsteak tomatoes or cherry tomatoes? Why?

Describe your style today in two words.

A billionaire is creating a new country on a Pacific island. There is a contest to name it. What is your entry?

A group of kindergarteners asks you the secret to a
happy, successful life.
What do you tell them?

And are you living that way yourself?

You're a hard-core vegan who's been offered $100K
to eat a steak at Ruth's Chris by a reality TV
producer. Your response?

Describe the water temperature over time in your
ideal shower or bath.

You're an alien anthropologist visiting Earth in disguise. Describe your first visit to:

Las Vegas

A sumo wrestling match

The Grand Canyon visitors' center

An animal shelter

Think of the best career you can possibly imagine, and write the reasons why you would be qualified for that job.

Now think of the worst career imaginable, and write your qualifications for that job, too.

A phrase you'd sew into the lining of
a wedding dress

A wildly inappropriate condolence note

Peek in a neighbor's window. What objects
do you notice?

Write an ad to sell an item that in your heart you don't really want to part with.

Walk outside. What is the third thing you notice?

What is in the shoebox under your grandparents' bed?

Write the ad for an expensive new drug that
improves bad posture.

Now, list the possible side effects.

In the United States, the Department of Transportation is in charge of time zones. You feel a new time zone should be created. Where is it, and what would it be called?

The girl voted "most popular" in your high school
class: Where is she now?

The boy voted "prettiest eyes" in your high school
class: Where is he now?

A dog or cat breed you think should exist, but
doesn't (yet):

Write four nicknames for people you dislike.

Bumper sticker on a white stretch limo

You're walking on the sidewalk when a driver
texting on her phone careens toward you.
Write <u>two</u> very different outcomes.

1.

2.

Describe a physical dictionary to a teen who's never seen one.

Describe *spell-check* to the sad ghost of Daniel Webster.

Think about an event that happened while you were traveling abroad, and tell your story from a local's point of view.

As you are reading your great-grandfather's wartime journal, a scrap of paper falls out. On it is a one-line note written in his hand. What it says:

If you had to choose one object from your possessions (past or present) to symbolize your entire life, what would it be? Write a few sentences about that object.

You step into the street without really looking, and a bus zooms by, almost hitting you. What flashes through your mind?

Write a conversation between a mom and her child about death.

Rewrite "White Christmas" or another Christmas standard as a Hanukkah song.

Write a compelling marketing blurb for the most absurdly awful tourist attraction you can imagine.

You work for a major fast food franchise and you must market pizza-flavored water to the masses. How will you sell it?

You are a deeply sensitive, but socially tone-deaf, individual. You want to call off the wedding to your betrothed. In the most heartfelt way possible, send him/her the news via text—that is, in 160 characters.

Describe a serious world current event in the form of a limerick.

You have to interview the CEO of Apple on stage, in front of 800 people. After the niceties, what is your first real question?

A man lives in a big house with no family. He has one chair at the dining table. He owns only one set of silverware. Who does he meet?

Write the museum label
for an imaginary
painting, of any era.

Now write the label as
if you were a besotted
fan of the artist.

Write it as a snooty
academic trying to get
tenure.

Write it as the
painter's jilted lover.

Write about a song your mother sang to you.

Write the top four questions you wish your
ex would answer.

The first or last paragraph of the book you lack
the courage to publish

Write from the point of view of a character who has
taken a vow of silence.

Three reasons why bartering should replace money as the chief U.S. currency, beginning in 2015

Write the first line of a TV theme song; then, substituting one word for another of the same type (verb for verb, noun for noun, etc.), change it to something dark and troubling.

There's an abandoned, spanking-new Porsche idling
along a desert highway. You . . .

Write the first line of an anonymous e-mail to the
wife of the man you know is having a destructive
affair with your best friend

Write a paragraph from your ex's obituary.

Describe your favorite cereal—how it makes you *feel* when you eat it; no adjectives.

Write a news headline from the year you were born.

Write a headline from next week.

Write a headline twenty years from now.

A teenage girl has refused to speak to her mother, with whom she lives, for three years. Finally, one day, she comes out of her bedroom and says . . .

The toast you give at a wedding. You are secretly and hopelessly in love with the bride.

A postcard arrives. It was mailed 11 years ago.
It reads . . .

You stole your rival college's ceremonial bulldog
trophy. Write a ransom note.

Someone with the same name as you is revealed to be the President's mistress. You suddenly have a ton of new "friends" on Facebook. What do you post now?

You have to be at a big fund-raiser that evening, where name tags are necessary. What do you write on yours?

The scandal blows up for three more days. Where do you go and what do you do?

The long autobiography of a penny ends with this paragraph.

You're a police officer in a squad car on the night shift. One of your confidential informants texts to ask you to meet. The text:

Your 53-year-old character still remembers the phone number of the home she grew up in. What is the phone number?

What is the lesson you learned from your favorite book?

Regardless of where you were born, where do you feel like you're from?

Your eight-year-old needs to learn about the birds and the bees. What are your first three sentences?

Fill in the blank and keep going. "I really ought to eat more ___."

You live in a world in which everyone gets one word tattooed on their forehead. What's the word you pick?

What street sign would you like to create?

You're about to adopt a black dog with a white
streak on her face from the animal shelter. Write a
list of five possible names.

A coffee shop is opening on your corner. What's the
memorable tagline that gets printed on the cups?

What happened when someone shrank your favorite item of clothing?

Write about downsizing.

Recall that time you were humiliated in public.

You're given a one-minute, private meeting with the president. What do you tell him?

You are being held at gunpoint, and your assailant
says you have 10 seconds to make him/her change
their mind about shooting you. What do you say?

At her high school reunion, a woman is waiting in
the line for a drink at the bar when she discovers
a man she used to bully, and _____.
Describe four outcomes.

You've just found a cute apartment. But many people are vying for it. Write a few sentences to the landlord on why you are the best tenant in the world.

Take the worst movie you've ever seen, and write an extremely positive and pretentious movie review.

The proverbial cheerful family Christmas letter, written by a spouse whose secret New Year's Resolution is get divorced by summer.

Describe the brutal gang initiation rites for
a new mother's group.

For a book club

For a country club

Invent a legend about your hometown.

Invent a corresponding superstition.

Write a eulogy for a sandwich, to be delivered
while eating it.

Write three sentences imagining where these people
are today and what they're doing:

Your childhood
sweetheart

Your childhood
nemesis

Your favorite
babysitter

Your first teacher

If you could kill off one relative, who would it be?

Write a job ad in the style of a pretentious restaurant's entree descriptions.

A recently divorced woman got these three words tattooed on her clavicle.

You are suddenly unable to recall any words that are not proper nouns. Excuse yourself from a very formal dinner party without drawing much attention to this fact.

Tweet from a famous dead person

A new tagline for Vegas

A superhero creation myth set in colonial America

Someone is designing a museum about your life.
Describe one of the exhibits.

Write the sign on the wall.

You see someone walking a large animal that looks
like a dog, but could also be a pig.
What do you say?

Write an online dating profile for your 70-year-old
aunt who collects Hummel miniatures, salsa dances,
and, as described by your mother, is the
original cougar.